10 IMPROVISATIONAL FLUTE ETUDES
by Jeff Coffin

ISBN 9781734185386
Copyright © 2020 by Jeff Coffin. All rights reserved.
No part of this book may be duplicated or shared without the permission of Jeff Coffin.

Also available online as an e-book.
Special thanks to Josh Karas for his assistance.
Layout and cover design by Robert Hakalski.
Engraving by Kyle Gordon.
Back cover photo courtesy of Jeff Coffin.
www.jeffcoffin.com/flute

WELCOME!

I am primarily an improvising saxophonist but I also play quite a bit of flute and clarinet. While I'm not really interested in being a classical flute or clarinet player, I appreciate that the classical repertoire builds a strong foundation. However, finding non-classical studies to play that more suit my wants and needs are hard to find. I figured others might be having a similar issue so I made some up!

What you have here are ten improvisational flute etudes. **I have provided free MP3 streaming and downloads at www.jeffcoffin.com/flute** so you can hear and get a feel for the solos. If you want to play through them with backing tracks, I recommend getting the iRealPro app so you can change the various settings to your liking. If this is already a familiar musical language and style for you, choose your own tempo and just start playing. I recommend taking them quite slowly at first and eventually build them up to an excruciatingly fast tempo that makes your key joints smoke from the friction!! Well, I DO recommend starting slowly.

These solo etudes are improvisations I played using iReal Pro. I recorded into Pro Tools, transcribed my solos (tip: get the rhythms first if you're writing down solos), made some edits, put them into Sibelius, had someone fix the errors I made putting them into Sibelius, re-recorded them with the corrections and edits, and now they are ready to be played. Easy! :-)

I chose the chord changes to standard jazz repertoire that I thought would be familiar, beneficial, and fun to play. I think this book has something for everyone. And I named the solos just for fun.

Some of these might be pretty challenging but it's always good to have things to work on that take some extra effort. I wouldn't want you to be bored.

My recorded tempos are for example only so it doesn't matter if you play them slower to faster than I do. Find tempos that work for you and that allow you to sound good and execute the material.

I hope you have a fun time with these and that you learn some things along the way. I know I did. Good luck!

Peace, JC

jeffcoffin444@gmail.com
www.jeffcoffin.com/flute

TABLE OF CONTENTS

01 **Olive Mi** = All of Me
02 **Star Flies Like Star Pies** = Star Eyes
03 **Bluetude** = Blues (Bb & C concert)
04 **It's The Little Things** = All The Things You Are
05 **Mrs. Kowalski** = Stella By Starlight
06 **The Answer Is Yes!** = Confirmation
07 **The Jones Tones** = Have You Met Miss Jones
08 **It's Only You** = There Will Never Be Another You
09 **King Of Leaps** = Giant Steps
10 **Where My Photos At?** = Someday My Prince Will Come

"These flute etudes are going to be an amazing tool for my flute students. They are complex enough to keep our brains very engaged, and simple enough that classical players like us will not become overwhelmed by the harmonic language of these jazz studies. I am excited to integrate them into my curriculum!"

Molly Alicia Barth, Associate Professor of Flute
Blair School of Music, Vanderbilt University

"As a classically-trained flutist, these études inspire me to play/learn jazz! The imaginative and smooth solos fall nicely into the fingers, so learning vocabulary feels very organic. Jeff Coffin, a world-class educator, saxophonist, and flutist in his own right, opens a new window into his generous craft with this set of etudes. His audio tracks show the nuance of jazz phrasing that goes well beyond notation. Fantastic resource. Great job, JC!!"

Dr. Daniel Pardo, Assistant Professor of Flute
Prairie View A&M University
Yamaha Performing Artist and Clinician

"As usual Jeff Coffin — AKA the sax-student-whisperer — hits the high E# (#anomaly) for those of us who double on the instrument, but also for the serious classical flautist who has eyes to venture into the soul a bit more. These etudes/exercises give you the ramp on to the improvisor's freeway with less fear."

Kirk Whalum, Grammy Winning Saxophonist/Flautist

"I hear so many beautiful influences in here from Yusef Lateef to Herbie Mann's dark tonal palette. It swings, is joyous, has a sense of humor and educates all of us, from the pros to the novice. Thank you Jeff for sharing your light and joy of music and the flute!"

Jay Rodriguez-Sierra, Saxophonist/Flautist - NYC

Jeff Coffin has made a valuable contribution to flute pedagogy with his book of etudes. It is valuable on many levels and gives the player a good insight into basic jazz harmony. Enjoy!

Lew Tabackin, Jazz Legend / Multiple DownBeat Critics Poll Winner (Flute)
Multi-Award winning Jazz Flutist & Tenor Saxophonist

OLIVE MI
All of Me

Comp. **Jeff Coffin**

SPACE FLIES LIKE STAR PIES
Star Eyes

Comp. **Jeff Coffin**

fine

BLUETUDE
Blues in B♭

Comp. **Jeff Coffin**

BLUETUDE in B♭

BLUETUDE
Blues in C

Comp. **Jeff Coffin**

BLUETUDE in C

IT'S THE LITTLE THINGS
All The Things You Are

Comp. **Jeff Coffin**

IT'S THE LITTLE THINGS

MRS. KOWALSKI
Stella By Starlight

Comp. **Jeff Coffin**

MRS. KOWALSKI

THE ANSWER IS YES!
Confirmation

Comp. **Jeff Coffin**

THE ANSWER IS YES!

THE JONES TONES
Have You Met Miss Jones

Comp. **Jeff Coffin**

THE JONES TONES

IT'S ONLY YOU
There Will Never Be Another You

Comp. **Jeff Coffin**

IT'S ONLY YOU

KING OF LEAPS
Giant Steps

Comp. **Jeff Coffin**

-24-

KING OF LEAPS

WHERE MY PHOTOS AT?
Someday My Prince Will Come

Comp. **Jeff Coffin**

-26-

WHERE MY PHOTOS AT?

ALSO BY JEFF COFFIN

The Road Book
The Saxophone Book (1-3)
Jeff Coffin & the Mu'tet Play-Along
The Articulate Jazz Musician (w/Caleb Chapman)

Available at www.jeffcoffin.com

www.ingramcontent.com/pod-product-compliance
Lightning Source LLC
Chambersburg PA
CBHW081238080526
44587CB00022B/3985